DIG, DUMP, ROLL

For John. SS

First published in the UK 2020 by Walker Books Ltd
87 Vauxhall Walk, London SE11 5HJ

10 9 8 7 6 5 4 3 2 1

Text © 2018 Sally Sutton
Illustrations © 2018 Brian Lovelock

The right of Sally Sutton and Brian Lovelock to be
identified as author and illustrator respectively of
this work has been asserted by them in accordance
with the Copyright, Designs and Patents Act 1988

This book has been typeset in Anton and Block T

Printed in China

British Library Cataloguing in Publication Data: a catalogue
record for this book is available from the British Library

ISBN 978-1-4063-8503-8

www.walker.co.uk

DIG, DUMP, ROLL

SALLY SUTTON · ILLUSTRATED BY BRIAN LOVELOCK

WALKER BOOKS

AND SUBSIDIARIES

LONDON · BOSTON · SYDNEY · AUCKLAND

crash-a-rumble
smash-a-grumble
What's at work?

Here's a clue:

it will clear the ground for you.

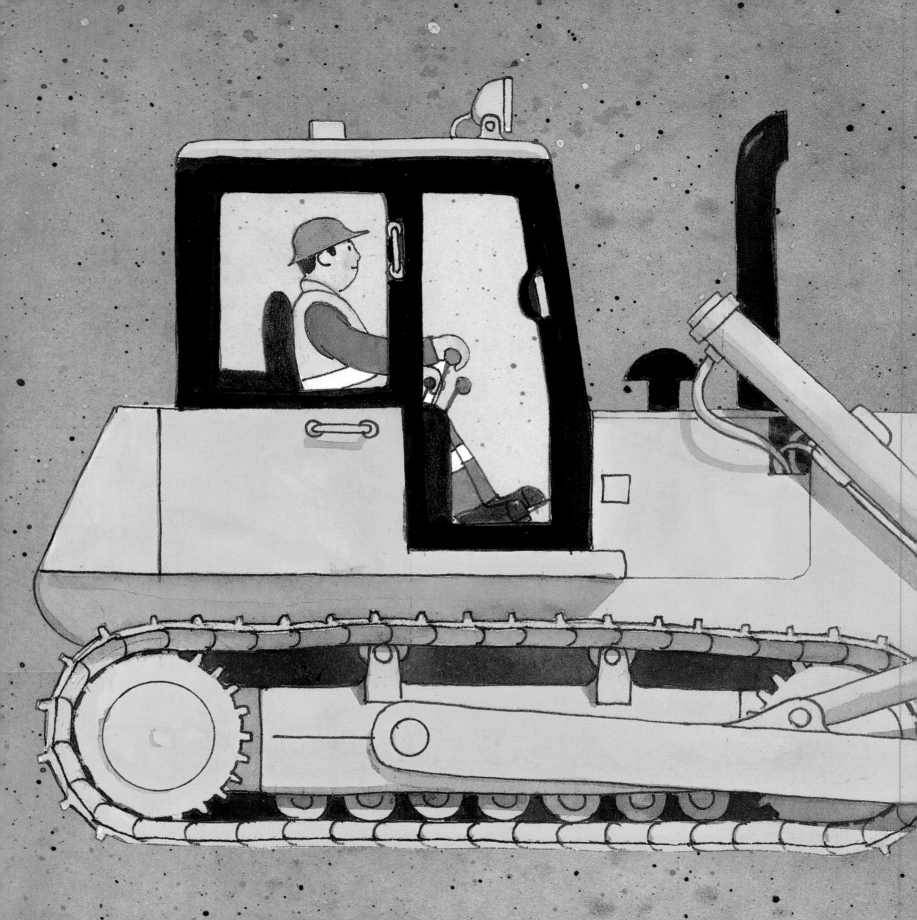

Bulldozer!

Coming through!

Bang-a-shudder
Clang-a-judder

What's at work?

Here's a clue:

it will
dig big holes
for you.

Digger! Digger!

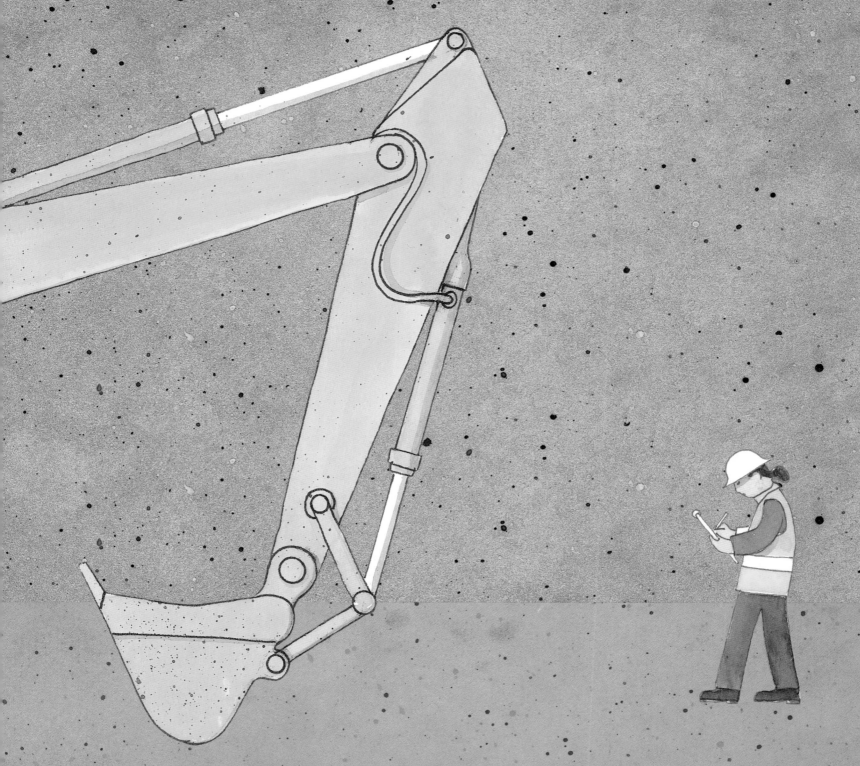

Coming through!

Slam-a-tippa
wham-a-slippa
What's at work?
Here's a clue:

it will
dump out
earth
for you.

Dump truck!

Dump truck!

Coming through!

squash-a-creaka
splosh-a-squeaka

What's at work?

Here's a clue:

it will
roll the
ground
for you.

Roller! Roller!

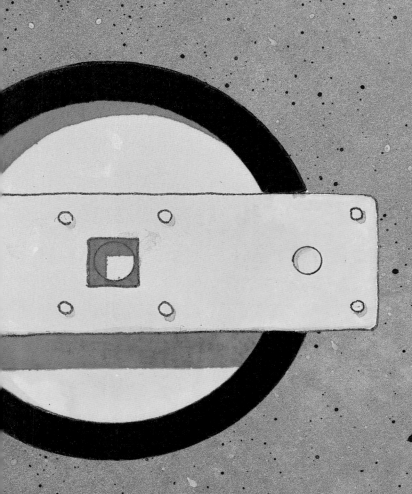

Coming through!

sploosh-a-splisha swoosh-a-swisha

What's at work?

Here's a clue:

it will
mix cement
for you.

cement mixer!

Coming through!

wham-a-hammer
Bam-a-slammer
Who's at work?
Here's a clue:

they will **build a frame** for you.

Builders!
Builders!

Coming through!

Skip-a-wiggle
Yippee! Giggle!

What's been built?

Here's a clue:

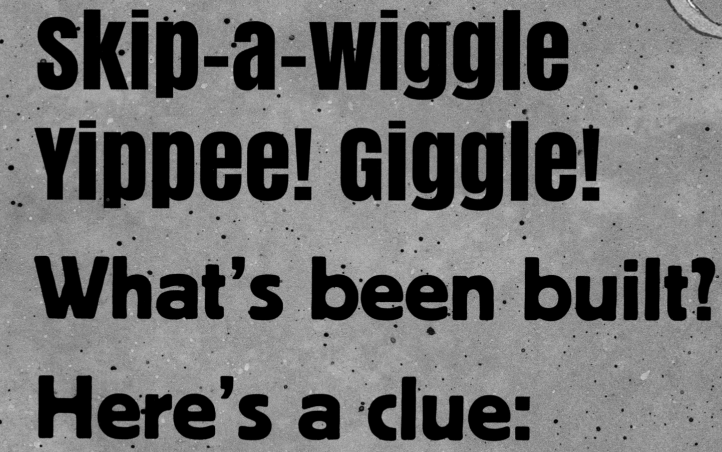

you can **learn and play** here, too.

School! School!

MACHINE PARTS

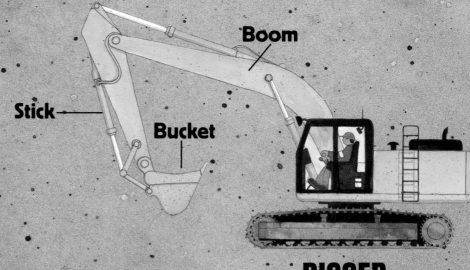

Boom

Stick

Bucket

DIGGER

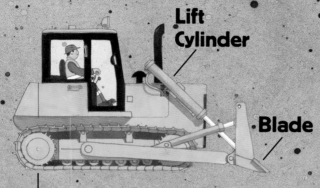

Lift
Cylinder

Blade

Roller

BULLDOZER

Drum

Main
Chute

Pedestal

CEMENT MIXER

Dumping Bed

Piston

Swing
Gate

DUMP TRUCK

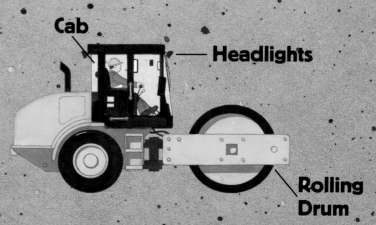

Cab

Headlights

Rolling
Drum

ROLLER